GOING CAMPING

by Harold T. Rober

BUMBA BOOKS™

LERNER PUBLICATIONS ◆ MINNEAPOLIS

Note to Educators:

Throughout this book, you'll find critical thinking questions. These can be used to engage young readers in thinking critically about the topic and in using the text and photos to do so.

Lerner Publications Company
A division of Lerner Publishing Group, Inc.
241 First Avenue North
Minneapolis, MN 55401 USA

For reading levels and more information, look up this title at www.lernerbooks.com.

Library of Congress Cataloging-in-Publication Data

Names: Rober, Harold T., author.
Title: Going camping / by Harold T. Rober.
Description: Minneapolis : Lerner Publications, [2017] | Series: Bumba Books — Fun Firsts | Includes bibliographical references and index. | Audience: Ages: 4–7. | Audience: Grades: K to Grade 3.
Identifiers: LCCN 2016023396 (print) | LCCN 2016035382 (ebook) | ISBN 9781512425505 (lb : alk. paper) | ISBN 9781512429268 (pb : alk. paper) | ISBN 9781512427462 (eb pdf)
Subjects: LCSH: Camping—Juvenile literature.
Classification: LCC GV191.7 .R63 2017 (print) | LCC GV191.7 (ebook) | DDC 796.54—dc23

LC record available at https://lccn.loc.gov/2016023396

Manufactured in the United States of America
1– VP –12/31/16

LERNER
e
SOURCE

Expand learning beyond the printed book. Download free, complementary educational resources for this book from our website, www.lerneresource.com.

Table of Contents

Camping Time

Camping is fun!

We spend the day

and night outside.

Adults set up the tent.

Kids help too!

Then they all set out their

sleeping bags.

Many campers go on hikes.

They see trees and other plants.

They can see wild animals.

What else do you think you can see while hiking?

Adults build a fire.

Some campers roast hot dogs

over the fire.

They eat at a picnic table.

What other foods could you roast over a fire?

The sun goes down.

Everyone gathers near

the fire.

People sing songs.

They tell stories.

Campers get to

roast marshmallows!

They make s'mores to eat.

Later the fire goes out.

It is dark.

Look at the stars.

They are very bright.

Why do you think stars look so bright when you go camping?

Now it is time for bed.

Everyone goes into the tent.

They get into their sleeping bags

and go to sleep.

The sun rises

in the morning.

Time to wake up!

Everyone cleans the

campsite before

going home.

Camping Supplies

tent

s'mores ingredients

sleeping bag

hiking boots

Picture Glossary

campers

people who camp

campsite

a place where people set up camp

roast

to cook something over a fire

s'mores

snacks made by putting a roasted marshmallow and chocolate between two graham crackers

23

Index

Read More

Carlson, Nancy. *Arnie Goes to Camp.* Minneapolis: Carolrhoda Books, 2012.

James, Helen Foster. *S Is for S'mores: A Camping Alphabet.* Chelsea, MI: Sleeping Bear Press, 2007.

Rober, Harold T. *Having a Sleepover.* Minneapolis: Lerner Publications, 2017.

Photo Credits